CH01457651

LEADERSHIP
LEARNINGS

FROM

CHHATRAPATI SHIVAJI
MAHARAJ

LEADERSHIP LEARNINGS

FROM

CHHATRAPATI SHIVAJI MAHARAJ

CYRUS M GONDA
DR. NITIN PARAB

EBD

EMBASSY BOOKS
www.embassybooks.in

LEADERSHIP LEARNINGS

FROM

CHHATRAPATI SHIVAJI MAHARAJ

First Published in India 2013

Disclaimer
While care has been taken to verify historical data and facts in this book, if there is any factual error, we request feedback from the readers for improvement. We are not qualified historians, and our intention in this book is to highlight the spirit of the leadership learnings from the noble and brave life of Chhatrapati Shivaji Maharaj, from which modern-day leaders can acquire and imbibe and improve themselves. Any improvements or corrections suggested by readers are most welcome and will be incorporated in the next edition of this book.

Published in India by:
EMBASSY BOOK DISTRIBUTORS
120, Great Western Building,
Maharashtra Chamber of Commerce Lane,
Fort, Mumbai - 400 023.
Tel : (+91-22) 22819546/32967415
Email : info@embassybooks.in
Website: www.embassybooks.in

ISBN 13: 978-93-81860-61-8

Printed in India by Decora Book Prints Pvt. Ltd. Mumbai.

शरद पवार
SHARAD PAWAR

कृषि एवं खाद्य प्रसंस्करण उद्योग मंत्री
भारत सरकार
MINISTER OF AGRICULTURE &
FOOD PROCESSING INDUSTRIES
GOVERNMENT OF INDIA

MESSAGE

This book 'Leadership Learnings from Chhatrapati Shivaji' by Cyrus M. Gonda and Nitin Parab is indeed a very unique endeavour of its kind. Chhatrapati Shivaji as an iconic historical figure of India has been a subject matter of many writers and historians, who have mostly projected him as a ruler, conqueror and a brave king of his times. His many achievements and exploits have become folklores which are highlighted in the book through many anecdotes and events during his life time. Cyrus and Nitin have focussed on the multi-faceted aspects of Chhatrapati Shivaji's leadership, enumerating his outstanding qualities and traits and have in a unique way brought their relevance to our present times in all walks of life. The thirteen chapters in the book very lucidly portray Shivaji's outstanding character that has been admired and respected in our country.

As a leader of his times, Chhatrapati Shivaji had indeed a deep understanding of his people and he communicated with them very effectively by addressing their physical and emotional needs and earned respect from them all. Despite the influence he wielded over them, he always visualized himself as a trustee of the kingdom. He is acknowledged as a great organizer and administrator who developed a unique participative system in which the support of the people to the administrative structure was built in by giving them a sense of contributing towards the welfare of the kingdom. He inspired people by words and brave deeds and practicing high noble ideals which he upheld throughout his life.

...2

Office : Room No. 120, Krishi Bhawan, New Delhi-110 001 Tel.: 23383370, 23782691 Fax : 23384129
Resi. : 6, Janpath, New Delhi-110 011 (India) Tel. : 011-23018870, 23018619 Fax : 011-23018609
E-mail : sharadpawar.sp@gmail.com

-2-

The efficient governance which he provided to his people surely speaks volumes about his skills. He had very clearly spelt out duties and responsibilities of the officials and institutions, which worked for the welfare of the people and provided them security. He also built and sustained a stable economic structure which ensured the prosperity of his people. He was a keen observer and had an ability to choose talent in others and entrusted them with work that were best suited for them. He believed in working for the empowerment of the people, irrespective of their religion, caste and creed and treated them, especially women, with great dignity.

As a military strategist, Chhatrapati Shivaji would certainly be considered among the best. His foresight and courage was blended with high sense of dignity confirming to the best traditions of statecraft. His conquests and valour was admired and respected widely because they were supported and founded upon universally accepted ethical values. He gave highest regards to the concept of justice and fair play. Shivaji was humble at heart and his receptive and open mind made him a keen and an enthusiastic learner, which helped him to embrace new ideas and techniques and blossom as a great leader. The authors of this book have very precisely highlighted these great qualities of Chhatrapati Shivaji and have perhaps for the first time shown how they are still very relevant in our present times.

My best wishes to Cyrus M. Gonda and Nitin Parab in this endeavour. I am sure the books in the series would be useful to both individuals, organizations and people in public life who aspire for leadership positions and would like to establish a legacy.

(SHARAD PAWAR)

Office : Room No. 120, Krishi Bhawan, New Delhi-110 001 Tel.: 23383370, 23782691 Fax : 23384129
Resi. : 6, Janpath, New Delhi-110 011 (India) Tel. : 011-23018870, 23018619 Fax : 011-23018609
E-mail : sharadpawar.sp@gmail.com

TESTIMONIALS

An excellent reference for developing a workable leadership style. The book highlights that the "Leaders" model is the way to proceed and shape a practical vision.

A hallmark of leadership is the ability to develop innovative approaches to carry the organisation to a higher rank. The writers remind us of the expectations of people who serve under the command of a leader. Overwhelmingly, people look for a forward-looking person who inspires and is proficient. The writers stress that a good leader envisions the future and enlists others to join in that shared vision. The book transcends the regular management approaches in favour of providing an interesting version on leadership and the expectations of staff under the command of a designated leader. The writers present a gallant vision for leaders to apply and follow. This book distinguishes from all others in emphasising what people expect from their leaders.

– **Vispi Rusi Bhathena,** *Chief Executive Officer, Bombay Stock Exchange Brokers' Forum* and *Dr. Aditya Srinivas, Chief Operating Officer, Bombay Stock Exchange Brokers' Forum*

The world is experiencing a period of deep darkness in the history of humanity and needs a Visionary Leader. I bless the creators of the Universal Leadership Series who have initiated this process of capturing Leadership Traits through their writings, trying to sow the seed of a new world order.

Let harmony, peace, good-will and good fortune prevail.

– **Chattobaba,** *Spritual Leader.*

This book must be read and re-read three times. Go through it the first time as a light story, you will love that part just like a kid reading an interesting story book. The second read will bring out the management theories around which Shivaji built and ran his empire, like a Corporate Head. The third time you will start connecting with your own management experiences and interweaving them with the teachings of these two management gurus – Cyrus and Nitin.

All in all, this is a must read by all who love management and leadership books. I can't wait for the next book in the Universal Leadership Series.

– **Vikash Mittersain,** *Founder & President, IBG India Business Group*

Very well researched and analysed from the management and leadership point of view. A must for Gen-Y to know more about actual strategic skills for combating in the corporate world. Great Stuff.

– **C. Subramaniam,** *President – HR, Siyaram Silk Mills Ltd.*

You have narrated real life stories and woven the theory of leadership and excellent management from the life of Shivaji. This I feel will be of great use to the individual who wants to know and study on how great leaders are born and made.

– **Lalit Kumar Jain.** *(Chairman, KUL, Pune)*

The book through its wonderful and seamless exemplification of overlap of leadership qualities possessed by the great warrior on one hand, and the traits required to become a great leader in the current context on the other, reinforces the fact that all the management principles prevalent today have their moorings drawn from Indian history.

The sense of fulfilment and accomplishment experienced after reading the book is unparalleled. I am sure that this book will ignite the fire in the minds of innumerable people and propel them towards perfection.

– **Dr M.G. Shirahatti,** *Chairman, Board of Studies in Management, University of Mumbai*

After combing through a vast repository of literature on Shivaji, the inspirational Indian leader, the authors of "Leadership Learnings from Chhatrapati Shivaji Maharaj", Cyrus M Gonda and Nitin Parab have presented here simple yet effective lessons from this leader's illustrious life to guide their readers to a lasting success.

This book is in effect a unique leadership development program. It can be used as an excelsior leadership development tool.

– **Manish Naik;** *Former Indian Army Major and founder of a boutique L&D firm, Dynamic Learning.*

I am sure this book will make a good mark on people seeking simple and lucid self-development inputs, as well as people who want to learn from the historical success stories of Chhatrapati Shivaji.

– **Ramesh Mitragotri,** *Chief People Officer; Aditya Birla Retail Limited.*

This book will serve as a handy tool in the hands of all people to learn from and implement in their lives these leadership principles laid down by Shivaji Maharaj.

– **M.R. Khambete,** *Chamber Of Small Industry Associations, COSIA.*

This book perfectly blends the leadership skills of the great nationalist icon, Shivaji Maharaj, with the requirements of today's workplace in terms of leadership traits and management practices. Through the use of 13 Mantras, an impeccable series of anecdotes are revealed, and their relevance for leadership learning for present day managers is established.

– **Mr. Yogesh Mohan Gupta,** *Chairman of IIMT Group of Colleges , Meerut and Delhi.*

DEDICATION

*We dedicate this book to the noble
Chhatrapati Shivaji Maharaj, the glorious people of
the State of Maharashtra, and to our Motherland,
Bharat Mata*

ACKNOWLEDGEMENTS

We would first like to acknowledge the efforts and dedication of Mr. Nauzad D Irani, who has tirelessly worked on the layout of this book, and who has also developed the front and back cover design. He has provided us with intelligent suggestions and creative ideas, and we thank him for his contribution.

We are grateful to Dr. Shubalaxmi Acharya, Steve Fernandes and Hitesh Bhatt for their relentless support and timely suggestions.

We also wish to thank Mr. Sohin Lakahani, Ms Varsha Shah, and the entire team at Embassy Books for having shown faith in this book and this series. Embassy Books have always been at the forefront whenever books of a positive and life-improving nature are to be produced, and we are grateful for their support and valuable contributions.

PREFACE TO UNIVERSAL LEADERSHIP SERIES

In the pursuit of the Science of Management, we have neglected and lost the Art of Leadership – Dr. Nitin Parab, Cyrus M Gonda

Leadership at all levels is a fine art. And like any art, it needs to be nurtured and mastered through a process of contemplation, reflection and practice.

The primary task of a leader is to bring a feeling of goodness into the people he leads. A true leader creates a renaissance – a reservoir of positivity that frees the best in people and allows them to achieve extraordinary results.

In these times of rapid change, 'Good Leadership' is what every organisation needs and looks for. Leaders who can visualise the future and make their organistion adaptive to change are the need of the hour.

Cyrus and Nitin have formulated the 'Universal Leadership Series' to bring about a thought process which will motivate, inspire and guide young leaders. The Series studies the learnings from great leaders from all fields – Military leaders, Leading Corporate Brands, Political leaders, Spiritual leaders, Leaders from the world of Sport, and so on. The learnings are based on interesting anecdotes and presented in clear and contemporary terms, which are easy to relate to and implement in the reader's organisation and personal career.

– Cyrus M Gonda, Nitin Parab

PREFACE TO BOOK – LEADERSHIP LEARNINGS FROM CHHATRAPATI SHIVAJI MAHARAJ

Chhatrapati Shivaji Maharaj is an icon, especially to the people of Maharashtra and India.

In a very short span of 53 years, he was able to establish the concept of Swaraj and also an Empire which extended throughout most of Western and Southern India.

His administrative skills are legendary and his vision and implementation of a well governed state adorn the pages of glorious history.

We authors have attempted to highlight his exceptional leadership skills in a very simple and fluid manner. We have highlighted the special incidences and anecdotes from Shivaji Maharaj's life and explained the modern leadership principles they relate to.

This is a great book for all those who wish to understand and pursue leadership thoughts and a leadership role by practicing the learnings enumerated herein into real-time action for success in their career and their corporate life.

We wish the readers to take the seeds of leadership thought and evolve as great visionary leaders for their stakeholders and organisations to benefit from.

Jai Maharashtra

Jai Hind

Cyrus M Gonda, Nitin Parab

CONTENTS

mantra
one

DEVELOP
EMOTIONAL
QUOTIENT

LEAD WITH EMOTIONAL QUOTIENT –

CONQUER THE HEART

ANECDOTES FROM SHIVAJI'S LIFE

People in general are not complicated.

Most people are simple, honest, and direct.

And they prefer to be addressed and treated in a simple, honest, direct and uncomplicated manner.

Shivaji, right from the early years of his life, when he was growing in strength, addressed his people in a language that was spoken simply and addressed directly to their heart.

This was possible because Shivaji himself thought and spoke with the human qualities of honesty and integrity.

By doing so, he was able to ignite ambition in the common people, making them excel in their efforts and perform extraordinary deeds.

Shivaji planned and participated in many strategic battles and campaigns, yet he always found time for the poorest and weakest of his subjects who came knocking at his doors for help or justice. This was because Shivaji **empathised** with them, could feel their pain, and wanted to do his utmost to emotionally bond with all his people.

Being part of Shivaji's team, the people felt from their hearts that they had found the true leader who would bring genuine goodness into their lives. Their hearts, feelings and emotions, even their dreams, were understood by and synchronised with those of their leader, Shivaji.

To demonstrate how Shivaji empathised with the emotional needs of his team, the following example will throw light.

One of Shivaji's captains was once on a military expedition where he had to prolong his stay more than had been expected to obtain the desired results. During this period, the captain's son was scheduled to get married and the wedding preparations were under way. Shivaji personally saw to it that all arrangements for the wedding were looked into with great detail.

He also attended the wedding and showered

blessings on the young couple.

In this manner, the absence at the wedding of the father of the groom was diluted, and Shivaji's personal presence created a positive emotional experience for the entire family and guests.

Many such examples exist of Shivaji understanding that his people all had their individual emotional needs, and he gave sufficient time and energy from his busy schedule to connect with his followers emotionally.

This raised his esteem in the eyes of his people and made him an even greater leader to look upto.

Experience is the mother of all wisdom. Shivaji grew wise with experience. Having led many individuals on the path to victory, his experiences of multiple war and peace time situations shaped him into a noble and just ruler. Because of his experience in helping the people with the difficulties they faced, he was able to empathise with them.

He could do this as he had led from the front, establishing the vital emotional connect.

He was able to combine the brilliance of a well-developed strategic mind with true and genuine human feelings, thereby creating a chord of oneness with his people. It was this emotional chord and connect that was instrumental in making his people follow him readily with full trust and faith. The pages of history are filled with glorious incidents where people have even willingly sacrificed their lives when the organisation needed it the most, knowing fully well that the organisation and its leaders would take good care of their families.

Shivaji could ignite such patriotic passion lying within the people and make them march ahead together for a noble cause.

When Shivaji entered the state of Hyderabad, then ruled by the Nizam, the scene is described where he rode in front of his troops and the watching crowd were eager to see his smiling face, having heard the great stories about this great man.

Although it was a difficult occasion for him, as Hyderabad was an unknown environment, the people looked up to him, showering him with gold and silver petals, on the basis of what they had heard about his leadership style as a people's leader. Shivaji did not disappoint them, keeping a smiling face and acknowledging their welcome gestures, and he succeeded in healthy victory in negotiations with the Nizam of Hyderabad, primarily because he had the people of that city on his side. Shivaji, though undisputed king, did not think of himself as the owner of his kingdom, but rationally realised that he was a trustee for future generations and serving his people.

Shivaji's spiritual *guru* was Ramdas Swami, one of the greatest saints of Maharashtra. After capturing Satara, Shivaji erected an *Ashram* (Monastery) for his *guru* in the neighbouring hill fort of Parli (Sajjangarh).

It always puzzled Shivaji why his *guru* Ramdas Swami would still go out daily on a begging tour, though his royal disciple had provided him with all possible amenities, facilities and wealth.

Shivaji decided one day to place at the feet of his *guru* a deed, a certificate, making a gift of all his kingdom to the *guru*. Ramdas Swami gracefully accepted the gift and appointed Shivaji as the caretaker of the kingdom on his behalf and bade him to rule the kingdom not like an owner or an autocrat, but like a trustee, responsible for all his acts to the higher authority of the Divine Lord himself.

Today, the concept of *'Servant Leadership'* is an evolved concept in management thought. This concept becomes attainable when the leader reaches a high level of maturity and thinks beyond himself and his personal benefits. He starts looking into the extended eco-system and eco-circle of his colleagues, departments, suppliers, customers and all stakeholders.) Shivaji developed and practiced and put in place this evolved aspect of management leadership, 300 years before western management practitioners conceived it.

Shivaji then made the red-saffron colour of the Hindu *sanyasi* his flag, known as the *Bhagwa Zenda*, or the Saffron Flag. This signified that he fought and governed in the name of the Lord. Thus came upon him the title – *Jaanta Raja*, or 'Conscious King' or the 'King that knows all and does all for the betterment of his people.'

In this way, he knew and understood and empathised with the very pulse of his people, thus making him an emotionally mature leader, loved and respected by his loyal subjects.

LEADERSHIP LEARNINGS

In the cold and sometimes friendless atmosphere of organisational life and ruthless commerce, the rare, true leader brings in warmth and human feelings into the lives of the people of the organisation.

The true leader addresses people on the human grounds of love and compassion, thereby creating a solid community feeling among the members of his team.

He is truly empathetic towards his people, putting himself in their position and in their shoes, and encourages and motivates them to perform to the best of their strengths. He also understands the weaknesses of his people and does not criticise them, but helps them to overcome these weaknesses and develop as evolved human beings.

It is not that by putting his people first, that he ignores the needs and objectives of the organisation.

Rather, once this emotional bond is established, his team is ready to perform extraordinarily. Thus, ordinary people working in organisations raise their level of functioning when led with vision, purpose and empathy.

The true leader, by leading with the heart, brings about peace, harmony and a conducive working environment, thereby reducing conflict and ushering in goodwill and good fortune throughout the organisation.

Human beings are social creatures by nature. As communities of like-minded individuals get formed at the work place, regular interventions of top management (core committee), need to take place, so that the workforce at large feels included in the collaborative growth of the organisation.

Only when the people start feeling emotionally attached with the organisational activities which they undertake, will superior performance standards which are well above the average be achieved.

If work is done mechanically and as a matter of routine, then mental lethargy and stagnation set into the thinking process, leading to performance decay.

Even good performers will get trapped into this decay and will not contribute as expected.

It is vitally important that a leader takes time to understand the problems and difficulties, both professional and personal, that the people at the lowest grass-root level of his organisation are facing.

This is also a very fair and just way to lead. Too many so-called leaders today leave this important job to others down the line, without having trained them to look after the emotional needs of themselves or their subordinates, or supervising their efforts. For such leaders, people have been reduced to commodities and mechanical robots. This lack of empathetic human behaviour from the leader has seen many a potentially sound organisation bite the corporate dust and crumble. It also results into discontent and resentment at the grass-root level, and organisational work also suffers.

Any leader who is genuinely concerned about the physical and emotional welfare of his people and who commits time and other resources and takes action to ensure their well-being will always succeed, leaving behind an impact which would be a guiding signpost for future generations of leaders, who would clearly see the path ahead, and be inspired to successfully follow it.

ACTION POINTS

FROM

"mantra one"

FOR YOU TO PRACTICE

1. Empathise and speak aloud with your heart

   - That is the purest language

2. Sympathise with the less fortunate and be in harmony with nature

   - Your path will become easier

3. Positive emotions resonate and bring people together in synergy

   - Practice developing a positive attitude

4. Win the hearts of your people by acts both great and small

Your Insights...

mantra two

MERIT - YOUR KEY TO RECRUITMENT AND PROMOTION

MERIT – THE LEADERSHIP KEY TO SUCCESSFUL RECRUITMENT AND PROMOTION

ANECDOTES FROM SHIVAJI'S LIFE

Shivaji believed very strongly in the power of merit.

All key posts were filled by him on merit, not on the basis of caste or religion.

Most individuals in Shivaji's army were brought in through the 'referral system', which even the corporate world today has recognised as being the most advantageous. It ensures that posts are filled on recommendations by your already trusted people, who know the type of individuals your organisation would require, and the background check is already ensured by the person who is recommending the new recruit. This system also fosters a feeling of oneness and brotherhood throughout the organisation.

At the same time, Shivaji personally interviewed

people for selection at middle and senior levels and tested them not only on their skill to do the job, but also evaluated their character and loyalty.

Thus Shivaji knew his people well before he selected them for key middle and senior level positions, which is why he could count on their abilities to take the organisation forward at the right pace and also depend on their loyalty in times of crises. Automatically, since he personally was acquainted with the strengths of the various individuals, he could place the right person in the right job.

Also, in Shivaji's army, there were two categories of employment which were practiced. One category of people, were the full-time employees on a salaried basis. They formed the backbone of the army.

The other category were employed on project or assignment basis, who performed military duties when there was a need. In peace time, they worked as farmers, and when needed they joined in military campaigns and were paid accordingly. By developing this system, Shivaji demonstrated great intelligence in keeping both a full-time as well as a readily available part-time force. In the selection of both, Shivaji was personally involved and kept merit as a prime criteria.

Shivaji's royal gift and talent for judging and evaluating character was one of the main reasons for his success. His selection of generals and governors, diplomats and secretaries, was never at fault. **This made him one of the most able administrators in history ever to run a kingdom**.

Shivaji had developed through practice a great knack of utilising the right people for the right job and industry.

Society develops due to technological advances. But food still remains the basic requirement of any society. Food production comes first, then its distribution, and then revenue generated from its sale accrues to the state.

Shivaji identified and utilised the services of the *Kumbi* clan (farmers) and the *Malis* to cater to the food requirement of his kingdom.

Similarly, the sea-faring socio-economic groups like the *Bhandaris,* the *Kolis,* and the *Agris,* were selected to create the expertise of the navy. Their knowledge of fishing, tides, sea-currents, weather, storms, boat-making, etc., were effectively channelised, and Shivaji developed their talents and encouraged their inherited skills to greater heights.

Similarly, the *Tambolis, Rangaris, Suthars, Lohars* and

so on were systematically selected and engaged in the process of creating the great Maratha empire, as they had the natural skills in their own area of expertise and domain and contributed whole-heartedly. In this manner, Shivaji made them feel special as part of a cohesive whole, and engaged them in contributing to and sharing in the fruits of the great kingdom he established.

The Engagement, Empowerment, Co-creation and Collaborative theories which are spoken of so highly today in elite management circles, were put into practice and adapted in creating an organisation based on merit, purpose and commitment by Shivaji Maharaj over three centuries ago.

Looking at the ramparts of hilly forts such as *Shivneri, Panhala* and *Devgiri,* it is obvious that only under harsh conditions and with the right use of skilled manpower could such forts have been constructed under Shivaji's able guidance of selecting the right set of people for the various specialised tasks.

Mountains exist everywhere in the world, but forts of such grandeur and magnitude can be seen in very few regions. It speaks highly not only of the foresight, but also of those hands which chiselled such hard rock like basalt, which is hard to crush even with the help of dynamite. One can visualise the power in the wrists and the refinement of the mind of the people engaged and motivated by Shivaji in the successful completion of this arduous task.

It also speaks of the high knowledge of metallurgy being used by Shivaji to create one of the favourite weapons of his army, the *Dandpatta* – a long sword used by his warriors.

Thus, one can see and understand the strong knowledge base pursued and persevered in by Shivaji to establish righteous rule and to build a formidable empire.

All this was possible, because Shivaji understood whom to deploy for the right task, thus bringing out superior results by utilising innate skills and talents of different individuals.

LEADERSHIP LEARNINGS

Ask any well-balanced and mature CEO what is the starting point of success. **He will say that it is selecting the right person for the right job.**

When bias or lethargy creep in while selecting individuals for key organisational posts, quality and organisational reputation get diluted.

It requires self-discipline and the ability to be assertive and say 'No', and not succumb to bias, influence or pressure to select an inappropriate person for a key post. It is natural that leaders, being human beings, display a certain amount of bias towards their chosen favourites in selection and promotion, but Shivaji demonstrated that a good leader can rise above it through self-discipline.

It is not necessary that you need to be at a top management level to participate in the recruitment and selection process of your organisation. All managers have some level of say in staff selection and in the recommending of suitable candidates. Take this opportunity at the early stage of your career to develop the expertise and self-discipline you will need to succeed when you occupy a senior decision making position.

But being unbiased while selecting individuals does NOT mean that you go to the other extreme by deliberately ignoring family members or friends, even though they are meritorious, Don't go to extremes to prove your fairness. That is not correct either. If a friend or a family member prove themselves to be capable and appropriate for a role, by all means appoint them.

Of course, family members of existing leaders often have a logical and biological advantage in being selected for the right reasons as they have been living closely with the leader and absorbing the culture, character and issues relating to the organisation, as well as the value systems of the leader.

So it is not that a close family member of the leader should not be selected for a key post. If meritorious, he can and should be chosen. There should be no bias against him just because he is related to the leader.

But the key word is 'merit'.

Corporate leaders need to involve themselves personally in the hand-picking of candidates, especially for key middle and top level posts in their organisation, and not leave these decisions in the hands of outside recruitment agencies alone.

Leaders need to remain hands-on in the process of recruitment, thoroughly understanding the strengths and limitations of any individual, before taking him on board in a decision-making role in their organisation.

With the right man in the right place, a major part of the leader's job is done.

ACTION POINTS

FROM

"mantra two"

FOR YOU TO PRACTICE

1. Understand the importance of having the right people in the right place
   – Promote on Performance

2. Know and thoroughly understand the person whom you are recruiting to be a vital part of your valuable team

3. Understand how human behaviour works, as it is the essence of success in all strong brands – Every great leader needs to also be a psychologist

4. Build strong networks to attract the right people to your organisation
   – Once they join, take all efforts to motivate and retain them

Your Insights...

_____

_____

_____

_____

_____

_____

_____

_____

_____

_____

_____

_____

mantra three

BUILD TRUST THROUGH EFFECTIVE COMMUNICATION

BUILD TRUST THROUGH EFFECTIVE COMMUNICATION – WALK THE TALK

ANECDOTES FROM SHIVAJI'S LIFE

Shivaji Maharaj, in his inner mind, right from a young age, visualised an empire which would be primarily based on the philosophy of *Dharma* (righteousness).

The stories told to young Shivaji by his mother during his formative years instilled in him the concept of a righteous and a just society.

Shivaji was definitely a powerful and inspiring orator and communicator. This brought his people close together and closer to him. A strong, unified bond was created. This quality of being an inspiring orator is one quality that all aspiring leaders need to develop. No one is born as a good speaker. It has to be worked at, just like any other skill.

True oratory comes not from the tongue, but from the heart – **Cyrus M Gonda, Nitin Parab**

Shivaji truly **FELT** what he said, which was why he was such an effective communicator, and which was why his people trusted him.

He used to regularly address his *Malwas* (troops), always encouraging them to lead a life of honour and dignity. He himself set the example for them to follow in this regard.

Men followed and respected him and loved him, primarily because they trusted him. They knew that true justice could be obtained at his court due to his fair, just and benevolent character and his inspirational deeds.

A man may be a good speaker, a sound administrator, charismatic, but people will not love and respect him till they can trust him – **Cyrus M Gonda, Nitin Parab**

Shivaji did not just make speeches to the public and then practice something different in his own life. **He practiced what he said, and he was the first to set the good example in all respects; he never expected others to do what he himself did not practice.**

Many people are GOOD SPEAKERS, but they do not become GREAT COMMUNICATORS till they can walk the talk – **Cyrus M Gonda, Nitin Parab**

Shivaji was a thinker, a strategist, and a great hands-on leader, who could inspire victory in the minds of his people, because he led them from the front.

Because Shivaji was honest with his people, there was no internal revolt ever during his entire reign, which shows the complete trust people had in his leadership, which can never come through fear, but only through respect. This is the quality which all leaders need to develop.

Shivaji was honest in his dealings with all, which is why he increased his standing as a great leader.

LEADERSHIP LEARNINGS

Many people in leadership positions today are very good at using flowery language. They go to public speaking classes and learn to speak confidently in front of an audience.

But the one thing which many of these individuals lack is the trust of their followers. This is why they remain incomplete leaders, not full leaders. We term this as 'HOLLOW LEADERSHIP'.

It is essential that the people whom you lead, need to believe that what you say to them is true and correct and that you have the organisation's interest at heart when you say it.

A good leader needs to learn to match his actions with his words.

The great leader has to have an element of passion ingrained with deep insights, learning and commitment, to inspire ordinary people to carry out extraordinary tasks. This after all, is the true purpose of leadership.

In today's world, leaders try to out-perform each other in their speech and give false commitments.

No follower can trust such a person and no person can become a true leader in this way.

Aspiring leaders should learn from Shivaji's example and aspire to attain the type of honest communication which he perfected. Even if the truth he had to tell his people was bitter, it never entered his noble mind to speak anything but the truth.

The reward that Shivaji received for this honest communication was the love, respect and trust of his people, which is the highest reward that any true leader can ever hope to gain.

If trust is the foundation of great leadership, it is based on the integrity of the individual, which is easily noticeable over time.

Integrity is witnessed when the line of thought and speech is aligned with the line of action the individual undertakes.

People are keen observers of such issues and it generally becomes a topic for water-cooler discussions when the leader's speech does not match his actions.

In many modern organisations we have observed that the 'Vision' and 'Mission' statements of such organisations are not in sync with the path on which the leader takes the organisation.

Flowery words that form decorative frames on the walls of many a 'leader's' cabin, often have no bearing in reality, thus creating disconnect and discontent.

It is extremely important for leaders to articulate their Vision/Value/Mission statements with great thought and care, so that a unified message between word and deed gets communicated. This would channelise the people towards a specific purpose and a larger goal.

WORDS followed up by appropriate and synchronised ACTION should be the logical sequence a leader should follow while communicating, to steer the organisation and its people on a unified, common cause.

ACTION POINTS

FROM

"मन्त्र three"

FOR YOU TO PRACTICE

1. Trust is the one factor that lingers positively in the minds of your people

    – Do all you can to win their trust

2. Let your communication always be crystal clear with focused objectives

3. Always lead by example and not by mere speech

4. Remember, positive actions reverberate, recharge, and revitalise the atmosphere

Your Insights...

_____

_____

_____

_____

_____

_____

_____

_____

_____

_____

_____

_____

_____

mantra four

KEEP NOBLE PURPOSE OF ORGANISATION FIRST

IDENTIFY A NOBLE PURPOSE AND INSTIL PRIDE FOR YOUR BRAND AMONG YOUR PEOPLE – EVERYONE BENEFITS

ANECDOTES FROM SHIVAJI'S LIFE

The greatness of Shivaji lay in the fact that his objectives were never made for personal gain.

For Shivaji Maharaj – It was always Motherland and his people first and foremost.

The whole life of Shivaji symbolises the highest dedication to his noble purpose - His dedication to the Motherland. In fact, the way towards creating free India (*Swaraj*), was initiated by Shivaji.

His entire life depicts a journey driven by a single, selfless, noble-minded purpose and a focus on values which portray the highest glory of the human race.

Shivaji possessed a very high degree of self-esteem

and self-respect which he never permitted to be lowered or compromised at any level.

Even at Aurangzeb's court, when Shivaji as a guest of the Mughals was treated unfairly, he displayed utmost valour and courage, knowing very well that doing so could have cost him his life.

He did this simply because for him the self-respect of his kingdom was foremost and could never be compromised. Thus even in front of the powerful Mughals, in their own court, Shivaji bravely defied the unjust treatment he was given, as it would have negatively affected his position as head of an independent and self-respecting kingdom.

To make his people prosper and lead a life of dignity was always foremost in Shivaji's mind. Delivering true justice and ensuring fair-play for all his subjects became second nature to him to such an extent, that he even once had his own son punished for misconduct. By doing so, he established that it was justice foremost and nobody was above the law, and that the kingdom came first, always.

Shivaji through his visible actions of nobility of purpose, developed pride among all Indians in **Brand India,** 300 years ago.

Shivaji gradually built up strength to reach his noble goal. After capturing a few strategic forts, his initial major military victory took place when he defeated Afzal Khan, who had been specifically deputed by Adil Shah of Bijapur to vanquish Shivaji.

It was at Pratapgarh where he defeated Afzal Khan, who had been accompanied by a very large armed force. This strategic victory announced his arrival as a great leader, and now people started looking up to him as their saviour.

Shivaji saw to it that the captured were treated with dignity and respect, and that ladies in the enemy camps were pardoned and released with grace.

As a leader, these concrete actions showed his people that Shivaji cared for the value of his organisational brand – *Swaraj*, above all else.

Such single-minded focus and devotion to a noble organisational goal went a great way in cementing Shivaji's position as one of the greatest leaders of all time.

As has been immortalised in the classic song *'Aao bachchon tumhe dikhaaye'* from the patriotic Hindi feature film *Jagriti*, the lines dedicated to Shivaji's devotion to his noble cause go as follow:

'Dekho mulk Maratho kaa,
Yahan Shivaji dola tha,
Mughalo ki taakat ko jisne
Talavaro pe tola tha,
Har parvat pe aag lagi thi,
Har patthar ek shola tha,
Bolee Har Har Mahadev kee,
Bachcha bachcha bola tha.
Veer Shivaji ne rakhi thee
Laaj hamaree shaan kee,
Is mitti par tilak karo
Yeh dhartee hai balidan kee'

Please listen to the song and watch the accompanying video if possible. It speaks of the high level of motivation that Shivaji inspired among his people to achieve the noble objective he had chosen as his life's mission.

LEADERSHIP LEARNINGS

Aspiring leaders should realise that if they hope to be great leaders in the future, their focus and efforts need to be channelised towards identifying, understanding, and achieving their organisation's goal. This process should also be transparently communicated to them through the philosophy and vision envisaged by the founders of the organisation.

If the organisation succeeds in attaining its objective, the leaders also succeed. This is a fact.

But it is not necessary that if the leader succeeds in attaining his personal goal, the organisation also succeeds.

So leaders should not look at their individual

success alone, but keep the organisational success and goal uppermost in mind.

If the organisation progresses, the leaders also progress.

This is what is called as Win –Win.

The Win – Win philosophy lies at the heart and root of effective leadership.

As we saw, Shivaji's efforts were never directed towards personal gain, which is why he is considered such a great leader.

All organisations have their noble purpose, whether it is about creating great products and services, delighting their customers, or some other goal. You need to understand clearly what the purpose of your organisation is, then do your best through your skills and efforts to help the organisation achieve its purpose.

If you do this with selfless dedication, your reward will surely come.

That is what the Law of Karma says, and the Law of Karma is the most dependable law in the universe.
– Cyrus M Gonda, Nitin Parab

Let us admit to ourselves. There is no harm in being a little selfish at times. We are all human beings after all. And, once we have done our best for the organisation, if we win as well and get our fair reward, without snatching or taking anyone's share. – that is the root of the management principle called as – WIN WIN.

Keeping the organisational objective uppermost in mind may be a little hard to practice, but it is not too difficult. Many great leaders have done so, and reaped the sustained rewards. Once an aspiring leader embraces this philosophy and follows this path, all around him will look up to him to take the lead.

Most organisations today are collapsing and failing because individuals in top positions in these organisations are looking out only for their own self-interest.

There is no common organisational objective towards which the efforts of all are being directed in a focused manner. This is why there are not many strong leaders visible on the corporate horizon today.

We know that Indian corporate executives have the potential to blossom. Now this latent potential needs to bear fruit. We need to see many strong leaders emerge on the Indian corporate horizon, and those who are reading this book and developing the qualities mentioned within will definitely be among those chosen elite.

If an individual can practice the quality of putting the organisation first, he will find himself elevated into the leadership role, leading to the creation of a sound and profitable legacy for himself and the organisation that he represents.

This quality was well displayed by Shivaji and this is the calibre of leadership we need in our country and in our corporate houses today.

Win –Win.

The organisation benefits, and automatically all the people and the leader himself benefit.

From this one vital, fundamental quality, all other winning attributes of leadership will follow.

Without this one quality, no matter how strongly an individual demonstrates the other remaining leadership qualities, such an individual's tenure at the top will always be short-term and shaky. Such a person will never be truly loved, respected or obeyed by his followers.

Put your organisation before yourself, instil pride for your organisation in your people, and the world is at your feet. **– Cyrus M Gonda, Nitin Parab**

As a leader, concrete actions are necessary to instil pride for your organisation among your people, but symbolic gestures, which convey positive meaning, are also very essential, as they resonate in the minds of observers, long after the action is done. This is how positive traditions are initiated and carried forward over the years, establishing the legacy of the leader who initiated them.

ACTION POINTS

FROM

"mantra four"

FOR YOU TO PRACTICE

1. Having a noble purpose gives you a clear direction to channelise your intention

2. Developing the right type of pride builds vital self-respect

3. You, together with your people, create and constitute your organisational brand

4. You truly win and succeed as a leader when your people proudly perform

Your Insights...

mantra five

DEVELOP ADMINISTRATIVE EFFICIENCY AND FEARLESS INDEPENDENT BOARD

DEVELOP ADMINISTRATIVE EFFICIENCY AND A FEARLESS, KNOWLEDGEABLE, HONEST, INDEPENDENT BOARD

ANECDOTES FROM SHIVAJI'S LIFE

Shivaji, apart from being a master strategist and warrior, was also an extremely able and sound administrator.

This dual quality is extremely necessary for modern leaders to understand, develop, and practice.

Normally we either have people who are good at leading from the front, but are poor at their back-end administrative work which is equally important, or the other way round.

But Shivaji realised the importance of efficient administration and gave it the time and attention it rightly deserved.

Shivaji established a strong government that included modern concepts such as a Cabinet of Ministers

(*Ashtapradhan Mandal*), a Minister for Foreign Affairs (*Sumant*), and also created positions for intelligence gathering.

When Shivaji took over the complete reigns of leadership at the age of 20, he created a team of officers who were men of tested ability and devotion.

Shyamraj Rangnekar was the prime-minister (*Peshwa*), Balkrishna Hanumant was accountant/ auditor-general (*Majumdar*), Sivaji Pant was Secretary (*Dabir*), and Raghunath Korde was Paymaster (*Sabnis*).

Shivaji thoughtfully created new posts to ensure flawless administration and added Tukaji Maratha as 'master of horse', in charge of cavalry.

Many kings in those days with warrior ability focused only on conquests and battles, but Shivaji rightly focused on consolidation of territory and administering it soundly.

With the right people deployed in the key positions, Shivaji was able to efficiently administer and control a wide and diverse kingdom.

Shivaji realised the importance of introducing benchmarks and standards for effective administration. The land in every province was to be measured and the area was calculated in *chavars*.

The measuring rod was 5 cubits and 5 *muthis* (closed fists) in length. A cubit was equal to 14 *tanus*. The measuring rod was 80 *tanus* long, which was = 1 *kathi*. 20 *kathis* = 1 *Bigha*. And 120 *bigha* = 1 *chavar*.

All areas were ascertained and measured in detail.

An estimate was made of the productivity expected from each *bigha*, 3 parts of which were left for the peasant to use and 2 parts went to the state.

Thus all lands were properly measured and the people felt a feeling of justice and not exploitation. There was no neglecting of this vital area by Shivaji, even though he was busy with battle campaigns.

Shivaji wanted to bypass the middle layer of revenue collectors and come into direct contact with the cultivators. Knowing that these revenue collectors were influential and financially strong and could create trouble for him, Shivaji still took this brave step for the good of his subjects.

Similarly, any good leader would like as few layers of hierarchy as possible, and would keep the welfare of his people uppermost in his mind. (Today, modern management theory advocates a flat organisation structure, with fewer layers of hierarchy, which is exactly what Shivaji developed 300 years ago).

Thus in an organisation, the communication of accounts should flow and reach from the top to the very bottom. Keeping the bottom-most layer in the loop of events and close to the top makes matters transparent and clear for all individuals. This improves trust and credibility. People will then be at peace, and productivity improves.

Due to his expert administrative ability and acumen, Shivaji could express his authority and make justice be felt throughout the land.

He established the most peaceful and prosperous time for his people against all odds. This was possible mainly because he focused on developing proper systems and procedures for efficient administration.

Shivaji went into great depth to create a structured hierarchy in his organisation for efficient administration, and for fixing accountability and responsibility. Each of these levels in the hierarchy was given clear job roles and descriptions.

For example, the Peshwa or the Prime-Minister, had the duties of:

- Looking after the welfare of the state in normal times.

- Representing the king in his absence.

- Keeping peace among other officers and resolving conflict.

- Promoting harmony among administrative personnel.

- Ensuring smooth flow in documentation and paperwork.

- Being a part of all official communications.

The *Majumdar,* or the Accountant/Auditor-General, whose duties included:

- To check all accounts of public income.

- To look into state expenditure.

- To counter-sign all statements of accounts.

The *Mantri,* or the Chronicler, who:

- Compiled and recorded the king's agenda for the day.

- Noted court proceedings.

- Watched over the king's invitation lists and fixed meetings.

- Guarded against assassination attempts.

The *Sumant,* or the Foreign Secretary, whose duties were to:

- Advise the king on foreign policy matters.

- Advise the king on war and peace.

- Maintain intelligence about other countries.

- Maintain dignity of the state abroad.

    (This shows that Shivaji did not just take arbitrary, autocratic decisions about declaring war and peace, but relied on sound advice from experts, trusting their judgement).

The *Nyayadhish,* or the Chief Justice, whose duties included:

- Trying major civil and criminal cases.

- Endorsing all judicial decisions.

- Passing judgement on rights to land, village and headmanship positions.

The *Pandit Rao,* or the Ecclesiastical (Spiritual) head, whose duties were to:

- Honour and reward learned priests on behalf of the king.

- Decide theological questions and resolve disputes on spiritual matters.

- Organise religious ceremonies.

- Be part of the committee on public morals.

This demonstrates that Shivaji was an extremely able thinker, and believed in sound systems and processes. The way he devised clear job descriptions for key posts is something which most organisations do not do so well, even today.

All this showed Shivaji's administrative acumen and organisational structural insights, which helped his kingdom run like a well-oiled machine, even when the king himself was not present.

Also linked with this leadership attribute, it is important for leaders to develop for their advice and assistance, a strong, fearless, knowledgeable, independent board.

Right from an early age, Shivaji was in the company of good and experienced advisors, who were wise, faithful and fearless, and who were able to channelise Shivaji's thought processes in the right direction. This in turn led Shivaji to seek huge levels of integrity and loyalty from the men he motivated and led. This was possible because Shivaji kept an open mind to learn from such advisors and also the strength of character to appoint and retain such advisors who were not mere yes-men and puppets, but also such advisors who would disagree with him where they felt he was wrong and who were not afraid to express it.

This too, is the hallmark of a great leader – the courage to have honest and fearless advisors and not mere **YES-MEN - Cyrus M Gonda, Nitin Parab**

LEADERSHIP LEARNINGS

The key to organisational success has always been to use fewer resources than your competitors, yet consistently win over them, as Shivaji regularly did.

Administration can be explained as - "the ability to control limited resources for good governance and derive optimum efficiency and streamlining in functioning."

Today, unfortunately, the domain of administration is often looked down upon by aspiring leaders as a clerical function. This is because administration does not appear to be a glamorous and exciting function.

It has been observed in modern organisations, that while leaders are giving their full attention to front-end, market-place battles and in developing competitive strategy, they leave no time, focus or attention to the crucial work of administration, which is neglected. **This leads to internal weaknesses, pilferage, scams, and then the organisation rots and ultimately collapses. Very like wood, which looks healthy from the outside, but is chewed to dust by termites within.**

The best-run and most profitable and most successful organisations today are the ones where the top management realises the vital importance of sound administration, and gives it the importance it so richly deserves.

All work of leadership cannot be glamorous and exciting. A lot of the work involved in leading an organisation is routine, day-to-day work, yet vitally important, for which systems need to be created, and monitoring and supervision of top and middle-management needs to be done. Else people at the grass-root feel there is no involvement and appreciation of their work from top-management, and the day-to-day work of the organisation suffers. When this happens, no amount of corrective measures can get back the ground that has been lost.

Shivaji realised the importance and developed the

skills of sound administration which he also put in place on the battlefield to secure many well deserved wins in battle.

In the function of administration, as a leader, it is important to focus your limited resources on your priorities and not dilute them by focusing on too many diverse areas ineffectively.

Shivaji understood this concept of sound administration very well. He revolved his clear strategy around building forts and training his soldiers for rapid cavalry movements. **Thus, he identified and played to his strengths and did not lose focus by doing too many things at a time, but focused on these two main areas and did them brilliantly well.**

In this manner he administered his resources efficiently and optimally, a lesson which leaders today need to learn well by focusing on not more than two or three key areas.

Shivaji, with his focus on his two main, thoughtfully identified, priority areas, maximised his productivity and was able to overcome the huge resource base of his enemies, who though they had far greater resources than Shivaji, were not so well focused nor efficiently administered. Modern research shows that the human brain is not designed for multi-tasking, but is capable of doing a maximum of four things at a time well.

Shivaji put into practice modern proactive strategic thinking centuries before it was formalised by management practitioners.

With such superb administrative skill and strategic thinking, Shivaji is ranked with the great generals of world history, such as Hannibal, Alexander the Great and Napoleon.

Also, in today's times when leaders are surrounded by Yes-Men, who are eager to tell the leader pleasing things to get on his good side, it is extremely important that aspiring leaders develop the habit of **keeping themselves away from such ever present Yes-Men, and keep as their close advisers individuals who do not speak merely to please the leader, but to give him sound advice, even though the words they speak may be bitter, as long as they are true.**

We often hear about the importance of developing the habit of saying a 'NO'.

Equally important is to develop the habit of LISTENING to a 'NO', without getting upset, especially when one is a leader **– Cyrus M Gonda, Nitin Parab**

Leaders of today should learn from Shivaji how to appoint the right professionals with the right bearings, knowledge, skill-sets and attitude to be a part of their core-team, and who would contribute purposefully to their board decisions.

This core-team needs to meet often, and deliberate the course of action the organisation needs to take and fine-tune from time to time. More than a mandatory annual affair, such meetings need to become quarterly affairs at the very least. In these meetings, all the core-team members should be physically and mentally present and actively participate, and the performance of the organisation and the organisation's behaviour and culture should be reviewed and monitored in detail.

With this review mechanism in place, there should be instant reward or instant reprimand of the people who undertake key organisational activities.

All these things, practiced so well and constantly by Shivaji, will make any organisation stay on the right course.

ACTION POINTS

FROM

"मन्त्र five"

FOR YOU TO PRACTICE

1. Do not ignore and avoid performing administrative work as being too routine, clerical, mundane and below the dignity of a leader

2. Avoid surrounding yourself with Yes-Men and sycophants

3. Encourage critical viewpoints even if they do not match your own thinking process

4. Develop a strong eye-for-detail

Your Insights...

mantra six

FORESIGHT AND VISION, VALUES AND ETHICS

ETHICS AND VALUES, FORESIGHT AND VISION

ANECDOTES FROM SHIVAJI'S LIFE

For both of us authors, the life of Shivaji symbolises the highest dedication to the Motherland and the path to creating a free nation (*Swarajya*), where people of all castes and religions could live together harmoniously to create a life of peace and prosperity.

In fact, the word '*Swaraj*' itself was coined during Shivaji's time and reign.

Imagine the brilliant foresight of the visionary Shivaji, envisioning a free and united India 300 years before independence was won. The spark of this united India was lit by Shivaji - a spark of freedom so strong that it burned brightly for 300 years before blazing into glorious song on 15th August, 1947.

The foremost attributes of a great visionary leader were well endowed within Shivaji. His vision of establishing an empire in his relatively short lifespan of 53 years, was a feat which few leaders in world history can ever equal. Constantly motivating his people forward and casting the correct impressions and values in the minds of his people was the art of great leadership displayed by Shivaji.

He himself led a life of frugal and simple means, thereby setting the example of - **'Simple living – High thinking'.** In fact when some Dutch visitors visited the kingdom and court of Shivaji, they were amazed to see a great king eating a simple meal of rice and *daal* (simple Indian lentil), on a plate made from banana leaves. **Indeed, simplicity is greatness.**

Shivaji loved his troops and ensured they were well treated and looked after, but, like a good leader, he ensured that in areas where values and ethics were concerned, strict rules were to be followed. Shivaji himself obeyed his own rules and set a good example by leading from the front. Some of the strict rules he laid down displayed the values that Shivaji held close to his heart. They demonstrate the nobility of his royal character and the fact that he led by values. Some of these rules he laid down were:

1. No woman was allowed to accompany the army. If any soldier was found violating this rule he was beheaded as an example for others.

2. No woman or child of the enemy camp was ever to be taken captive. Only male captives from the enemy side were permitted.

3. Cows (being sacred), were exempt from seizure and bullocks were taken only for transportation purpose.

4. No soldier was permitted to misbehave himself during a campaign.

Shivaji Maharaj once held a *durbar* (court), to mark the conquest of Kalyan. Gifts to commemorate the campaign were presented to him by various commanders. The commander-in-charge of the Kalyan camp, Abaji Mahadev, came with what he felt was a special gift. The 'gift' was the daughter-in-law of an official of the enemy camp, a beautiful girl. Shivaji stood up, walked up to the trembling girl, placed his hand on her head in blessing, and said 'I would like you to be my sister. If my *masaheb* (mother), had been as beautiful as you, I too would have been handsome.' He thanked Abaji Mahadev for finding him such a beautiful sister. He then ensured she was safely escorted back to her family with rich gifts.

Such was the greatness of Shivaji Maharaj. Although as a king he possessed supreme power, yet he did not misuse this power.

Shivaji could actually have authored – *'How to Win Friends and Influence People'* long before Dale Carnegie (the author of that book), was born.

Shivaji's strong affinity for sound values arose from his observation of lessons taught by his mentors.

The story goes that once Shivaji's mentor, Dadaji Kond-dev had made a rule that no fruits should be plucked by anyone for personal consumption from state-owned trees, as they were the property of the state. Once, while out on an inspection tour, Dadaji Kond-dev himself was tempted to pluck a ripe mango from a state-owned tree that he was passing by. Immediately realising that his act broke his own rule, he instructed his soldiers to chop off his own arm which had been responsible for plucking the mango and breaking the rule. His soldiers persuaded him to withdraw the harsh punishment he had set on himself, after which he declared he would give up eating mangos for the rest of his life in repentance.

This incident of the highest level of ethics from his mentor had a huge impact on young Shivaji's mind, and helped in developing his value systems through personal example.

Shivaji today is remembered as a great leader

and statesman. His conduct always displayed an unwavering adherence to sound principles of action and administration, which he had prescribed for himself as an adequate and necessary means to achieve his great cause.

LEADERSHIP LEARNINGS

A very important question which arises in philosophy is – 'What is Goodness?'

As the philosopher *Rafi* puts it – 'I think you never know how good you are until you have more power than maybe you should. If you're stronger than everyone else, or you have the power to put anyone you want in jail. If you have all this power and you **STILL** are gentle and kind and fair, then isn't **THAT** the test of how good you are?'

Shivaji's action in his respectful behaviour to the captured enemy lady is the equivalent of displaying the highest levels of respect, even towards one's competitors.

An organisation which displayed similar nobility in

the corporate world today would automatically win the respect of all players in its industry. Even the customers of their competitors would begin to respect them. Such an organisation would begin to be known and talked about as a **'Noble Organisation'**, which is the highest pedestal that any organisation or individual could hope to reach.

We all have heard and know that Shivaji was great.

But it is important to know that not only was Shivaji **GREAT**, but he was also **GOOD AT HEART**.

He truly followed the eternal Golden Rule – 'Treat others the way you would like to be treated.'

Ethics and values have come under the microscope in the corporate world in today's day and time. Ethics classes, which were an optional subject in the American MBA courses and going almost empty a few years ago, are today over-packed with students, eager to know more about this valuable quality of ethics after the recent corporate scandals which have taken place.

Defining what constitutes ethical behaviour when the moral fabric in society itself has been torn apart, becomes a very difficult proposition. Excessive greed, coupled with a one-dimensional selfish view, has seen many a leading institution collapse.

If educated people in positions of power could lie, cheat and steal for personal financial gain and never get reprimanded or penalised, the big question as to WHY one should be ethical in the first place arises.

In the classic Hollywood movie – 'Wall Street', the insider trader Gordon Gecko says – 'GREED IS GOOD'. With such thinking, the entire concept of ethical functioning is overshadowed and lost.

In the dismal gloom of our modern times, the bright light of ethical values shines brightly to show mankind the right way.

Whenever we see a person who has stuck to his values and belief-systems, his cause is celebrated, and society as a whole rejoices.

The ethical values which are the eternal pillars of a respected, righteous society help the leader to visualise a better world, where all benefit. They open the door to a holistic, stake-holder oriented organisation, which casts its impressions on the sands of time.

ACTION POINTS
FROM
"ℳantra six"
FOR YOU TO PRACTICE

1. Develop clear vision to achieve your chosen objective

2. Inculcate and practice the right values as early as possible to build a sound character

3. Ensure that ethics is your roadmap to sustained success

4. Remember, no great career ever takes flight without foresight

Your Insights...

_____

_____

_____

_____

_____

_____

_____

_____

_____

_____

_____

_____

Mantra Seven

IT IS NEVER TOO EARLY - TO LEARN TO LEAD

IT IS NEVER
TOO EARLY TO LEARN
TO LEAD

Anecdotes From Shivaji's life

Shivaji's glorious childhood was spent in the company of two great individuals who shaped his future and moulded his destiny, namely, his mother Jijamata, and his coach Dadaji Kond-dev.

Young Shivaji used to wander over the hills and forests of the Sahyadri mountain range, thereby conditioning himself mentally and physically to a life that was devoid of comforts and luxuries.

Camping in the valleys and moving along the mazes of the river valleys, young Shivaji hardened and toughened himself up to lead a life of strenuous exertion, to prepare for the leadership task which he knew lay ahead of him.

These early wanderings were not the mere aimless wanderings of normal childhood, but were contemplative and meditative in nature, and made young Shivaji robust, sturdy and strong-willed. They prepared him to successfully take on the role of leadership at a young age.

These purposeful wanderings also gave him early first-hand knowledge of the country and its people.

At a very tender age, Shivaji got together the local children and gave them a vision of a unified state, based and run on ethics and values. These early thoughts and talks sowed the seed of the great Maratha empire. Shivaji also displayed personal courage and valour, thereby casting the image of an emergent leader – a force to be soon reckoned with.

At the very start of his military career, he won victories against numerically superior and better equipped forces based on good leadership. This boosted the morale of his troops, creating among them a feeling of deep respect and admiration.

These early battles were comparatively minor in nature, but were essential for Shivaji to gain valuable experience and communicate the message to the world that he had arrived.

The young lion Shivaji beat the seasoned general Afzal Khan, thus transforming Shivaji at a tender age into a great warrior and leader. The news of Shivaji's victory spread far and wide, uniting his people under a common banner.

Thus, we see that Shivaji saw adversity and hardship from a young age, and successfully overcame them with utmost bravery and courage, and contemplative meditation.

He deliberately chose not to have an easy childhood, as he knew he was destined for a higher purpose. He did not choose to live a life of ease, though he could easily have done so, being born with a silver spoon.

Thus right from a young and tender age, Shivaji practiced the essential attributes of superior leadership, developing these attributes as part of his noble character.

Today, behavioural research studies have proven that the earlier an individual starts to practice any activity and develop it as an ingrained habit, the better and more skilled he becomes in that habit as life progresses. The same holds true for the habit and skill of leadership also.

This research with multiple relevant examples is beautifully explained in that excellent book – 'Talent is Overrated'. The case-study of Shivaji and his development of leadership qualities through sheer hard-work and dedicated practice from an early age would have been a welcome addition to that book.

LEADERSHIP LEARNINGS

The leadership lessons from the life of the young tiger Shivaji are very clear. They are also very important to understand and practice for any person aiming to succeed as a leader in corporate life, or in his own business, or in public life and politics.

Talent (which is inborn in an individual, as new studies suggest), is not as important for success as is the hard and consistent practice of any skill in order to master it.

Leadership is a skill, and can be mastered with solid practice, the earlier the better – **Cyrus M Gonda, Nitin Parab**

The earlier you decide your goal, and the sooner

you begin to practice the necessary skills to reach that goal, the sooner you will master it.

This is the basic rule to master any skill, and it applies to acquiring the skill of leadership as well.

Young people should take inspiration from the life of young Shivaji. At a tender age, when children today are barely out of school, Shivaji led armies and won battles.

This cannot be done by sitting in a chair and dreaming, but by going out into the field and understanding ground realities.

This early experience in leadership stood him in good stead throughout his entire majestic career.

Some people had questioned his leadership ability at an early age, but he proved them wrong. He had all the ingredients necessary to succeed – courage, determination, self-confidence, and an honest, clear goal.

He created his army from local people, training, motivating and taking them with him to a higher purpose.

Truly it is said – An army of sheep, led by a lion, soon turns into an army of lions.

So don't you worry if you don't currently hold a leadership position. Young entrants in corporate life should observe what needs to be done and just go ahead and do it. They should not wait to be told by someone. Show your superiors that you are ready to shoulder great tasks and are not afraid of hard work and responsibility.

Taking early initiative in life matters. It matters a great deal.

When one's life is pushed against a wall, many noble qualities emerge and carry the individual to new heights. This is exactly what happened with young Shivaji, and he chose the correct path. At an early age, he was thrust into situations that made him think and act like a true leader. The cruciality of the situation developed the noble instincts within Shivaji to face the innumerable challenges that came his way in later years.

In times of difficulty, some people break down, while other people break world records. Great leaders are born in times of difficulty and not in the comfort zone – **Unknown**

We all possess within us these noble qualities and leadership instincts. We need to listen to them, act on them, and bring them to the forefront by practicing them regularly, in a disciplined manner.

In his early days, Shivaji had to face internal opposition from other local chieftains as well as aggression from rulers of other states. Both these situations were handled efficiently by Shivaji, who displayed a wisdom and maturity far beyond his tender age, and won the respect of these chieftains and rulers. Practicing leadership skills on a regular basis made all this possible to a large extent.

It will work for **YOU** as well.

Provided you practice the leadership traits honestly, whenever you get the slightest opportunity to do so.

Don't worry. Higher doors will open for you soon. Very soon.

ACTION POINTS
FROM
"ɱantɾā ʂɛvɛn"
FOR YOU TO PRACTICE

1. Regular practice leads to perfection

   - So practice developing leadership traits regularly

2. Take personal initiative for your leadership success

   - No one else can be ultimately responsible for your success but yourself

3. Develop insight to identify your special talents at an early age

4. Establish a honest and fearless mind first and foremost

   - All other good things will follow

Your Insights...

_____

_____

_____

_____

_____

_____

_____

_____

_____

_____

_____

_____

_____

mantra eight

IDENTIFY RIGHT MENTORS - OPEN DOORS TO GREAT LEADERSHIP

IDENTIFY RIGHT MENTORS - OPEN DOORS TO GREAT LEADERSHIP

Anecdotes From Shivaji's life

In young Shivaji's time, the concept of a united India did not exist. His primary objectives right from a young age were to protect his people, ensure their safety, administer the land well, and deliver sound justice.

This noble vision of his was developed primarily because he used his sound judgement to learn from and to follow the advice of his two main mentors and well-wishers – his mother, Jijamata, and his coach Dadaji Kond-dev.

Both these mentors had a tremendous influence in shaping young Shivaji's mind and established the foundation of a great leader.

Being mentored by Dadaji Kond-dev, young Shivaji mastered the art of warfare and picked up the skills necessary to become an able administrator. It was then in his early teens, after being ably mentored, that Shivaji was given the responsibility of taking a serious view of his position as a future leader. It was Dadaji Kond-dev whom Shivaji looked up to, and who formatted Shivaji's mindset in a purposeful direction.

Ready and eager to be mentored, Shivaji learned and mastered the art of swordsmanship and the skill of administration at the able hands of Dadaji Kond-dev.

His mother Jijamata's good influence over young Shivaji made him develop an indomitable spirit and nurtured in him sound values and a strong character.

Shivaji's earliest mentor, his mother, also gave him a holistic view of life by narrating to him the great Indian epics, which instilled in him the ethical leadership qualities for his future role. For Shivaji's great and noble character to be well shaped and moulded, a sound moral mentor was absolutely essential to show direction of purpose.

Recent research has proven that it is the early experiences which we undergo, which have the greatest role to play in shaping our qualities and our character.

Shivaji intelligently kept himself in the company of older advisors who were wise and faithful and willing and able to channelise Shivaji's thought processes in the right direction.

Later in life, high levels of integrity and obedience were sought by Shivaji from the people he motivated and led.

This happened largely because Shivaji had been mentored onto the right path from an early age, when one's character is formulated and strengthened the most.

Thus credit is due to his sound mentors that Shivaji was able to flower into a successful leader at such an early age.

LEADERSHIP LEARNINGS

The learnings from these anecdotes from young Shivaji's life on mentoring are very important, both for corporate houses, and also for the young and ambitious individuals who join these organisations to make their careers.

Organisations today are very short of good leaders. Severely short.

Senior executives of organisations need to invest time and put themselves in a position to identify potential talent for leadership among the young individuals who have joined their organisation. A dedicated, structured programme should be established for this important purpose.

Once identified, these individuals should be

mentored and coached, and their minds should be conditioned to taking on gradually larger and more challenging responsibilities. When such support is provided by the organisation and its senior members, the young leader becomes courageous and confident to shoulder larger issues and opportunities which the dynamic world is constantly throwing up at him.

So everyone wins - the young leader who receives the gift of good mentorship, as also the organisation, which benefits by gaining good leaders to occupy key positions.

The task of establishing a structured mentorship programme is primarily the responsibility of the organisation and the senior people already present within it.

The lesson for the young individual who has entered the organisation is also very clear. However qualified he may be, he should realise that selecting, respecting and following a sound mentor is the true path to long-term career success.

Opportunity knocks at least once in everybody's life. Into all of our lives comes at least one good mentor who has our best interests at heart and has the capability and willingness to show us the right path. Learn to recognise this person when he enters into your life. **This too is a leadership skill that needs to be developed. This is the skill of developing good judgement of character.**

Just as in Indian tradition, without the initiation from the guru, the disciple does not progress, so too in the corporate world, without the initiation of a sound mentor, true and sustained success does not materialise.

There is a lot that formal education in school and college can never teach us. This gap in the practical education can be well filled by identifying and choosing and following and obeying the right senior.

As is rightly said, when the pupil is ready, the *guru* will appear.

Youngsters in the early stages of their career who wish to take on leadership positions sooner or later should realise that the time which they spend with a good mentor is very valuable.

We would also recommend the documenting and putting down on paper the process of mentoring as a move towards structured knowledge capturing for the good of the organisation as a whole. Thus the knowledge gained from one good mentor–mentee relationship would not be lost forever, but would serve as a learning point for future generations in the organisation.

As we mentioned, we firmly believe that every youngster gets the opportunity to be with at least one good mentor, who could come from personal or professional life. Few realise the mentor's immense value.

The mentor could come from anywhere, from any walk of life – a senior family member, a friend's father, someone in the neighbourhood, a teacher, or someone at work. So youngsters in the corporate world should make efforts to shoulder extra responsibilities and catch the eye and attention of seniors in the organisation, who will then surely invest time and effort in mentoring them to great success and glory.

The senior mentors would also take great joy in coaching a capable pupil, as through their pupil, their own wisdom lives on.

Alexander had Aristotle as a mentor.

Vikramaditya had Chanakya.

Shivaji was blessed with two mentors – his mother Jijamata and Dadaji Kond-dev. The list is endless.

We would love to see YOUR name being quoted as a great mentor in the future.

ACTION POINTS

FROM

"mantra eight"

FOR YOU TO PRACTICE

1. Identify, select and impress a worthy mentor to take you on as his personal pupil

2. Keep open eyes and an open mind when it comes to identifying a suitable mentor – the mentor could come from any walk of life in the most unexpected manner

3. For senior leaders, invest time in grooming and inculcating potential leaders into the philosophy of the organisation

4. Develop the crucial ability to gel with all age groups and people with diverse thought processes and learn all possible good from them

Your Insights...

mantra nine

OPEN MIND AND OPEN EYE — ADOPT NEW AND BENEFICIAL TRENDS AND TECHNOLOGIES

OPEN MIND AND OPEN EYE – ADOPT NEW AND BENEFICIAL TRENDS AND TECHNOLOGIES

ANECDOTES FROM SHIVAJI'S LIFE

Shivaji was born at a time when new discoveries and inventions were being rapidly made in the Western world. The style of weaponry was changing from the old era of personal warfare with swords and lances and moving towards the usage of rifles and cannons.

Shivaji was well aware of the technological changes taking place in distant lands and kept himself informed by constantly updating his knowledge and skills, and also acted early on this information to gain first-mover advantage (a very important concept in management today).

He created an efficient and modern army and gave them the best and latest weapons to arm themselves.

Shivaji, in a matter of ten years, from 1655 – 1665

became a formidable opponent and baffled the Mughal empire. The Mughals tried everything in their vast power to curtail Shivaji's advances, but he always remained one step ahead of them.

A great contributor to Shivaji's success as a leader was that he always had one eye kept firmly on modernisation of techniques, equipment and also ideas.

To Shivaji's credit, he created a superb modern navy for military purposes, unseen in India till that day. He had inherited only a small *jagir* (piece of land), from his father, but Shivaji expanded into coastal areas as well. Immediately on winning the towns of Kalyan and Bhiwandi, he started building ships of his own in the creek near these towns. He instinctively perceived that without the command of the coastal waters, his inland territories could not be safely protected, nor the economic prosperity of his subjects assured. Many pirates of different nationalities were at that time raiding and plundering the western coast and ports and looting and plundering at will. It was only a strong naval fleet supported by naval bases close at hand that could protect the western coast towns and the trade which was their life-blood. Shivaji made this his priority.

Besides this, Shivaji wisely planned to increase

his state's income and the wealth of his people by
developing overseas trade, and for this he established
India's first mercantile marine or merchant navy.
Shivaji was the first Indian king to establish a modern
navy under the stewardship of Commander Ambre.

Shivaji proved his faultless leadership by
constructing a number of naval forts on the West coast
to accommodate the growth of his fighting ships and
trading vessels.

Shivaji rightly invested in creating India's first naval
bases which were housed in his unique invention, naval
fortresses.

Shivaji also had to his credit the following naval
base stations – *Vijaydurg, Suvarn-durg* and *Jaygarh*.

It has been historically noted that the vessels built
in the Konkan dockyard region by Shivaji's naval team
could compete on equal terms with the best vessels
built in Europe at that time.

Truly, Shivaji was a pioneer in early adoption and
even innovation of latest technology and trends for the
benefit of his people and his kingdom.

**Right from a young age, Shivaji was involved
with education that shaped his thought processes and**

brought out the best in him. **Continuous learning was his strong point, and he readily learnt all that was good, beneficial and progressive, thus turning disadvantages into advantages and challenges into opportunities.**

Shivaji showed himself capable of **innovating as per the changing time and needs.** The cycle he followed was one of:

➤ Learn

➤ Unlearn

➤ Re-learn

➤ Experience

And back to learning.

And this cycle never stopped, thus creating a closed, continuous loop for life-long learning.

LEADERSHIP LEARNINGS

Old is definitely gold, but new is good too. — **Cyrus M Gonda, Nitin Parab**

Organisations today need to provide and protect themselves with the latest up-to-date technology and innovations. Only when appropriate technology and equipment and infrastructure is harnessed, will organisations be able to remain competitive in the new economy.

But using technology should not be a goal by itself and the people themselves should not be forgotten. People should always get priority over technology and modernisation. Encourage your people to move with the times, but do it in a humane way.

It is essential that leaders of today are ably geared up to capture and observe the latest trends and developments happening world-wide and become early adopters of the same, as this is essential for their organisations to perform better. Funds should be reserved and made available for such activities as and when required.

To create a well-balanced organisation, a good leader needs to have an open-minded approach. Being complacent with past achievements and dwelling on victories of the past will make organisations succumb to competitive pressures and they will soon find themselves redundant and out of favour and out of business. Leaders have to ensure they take the positive lead to ensure that their organisations do not fall into this trap.

A leader needs to take pains to explore and experiment with innovative ideas and practices. A leader who has developed a visionary eye, and has also practiced the open mind-set, can rise to the occasion and create a great, modern organisation that is sustainable, profitable, and people oriented.

In management terminology, corporate leaders need to follow the **LURE** principle, so ably demonstrated by

Shivaji. Today is the era of the Knowledge Economy, and Learning is a vital survival skill for corporate houses today, to attain and maintain the leading edge. Not just learning, but as Shivaji demonstrated, the ability to **Learn, Unlearn, Re-learn, Experience,** leads to success in innovation.

This involves:

- Learning in the present context.

- Unlearn, as the markets/customers/situations, demand.

- The need to Re-learn and progress with new methods and technologies to address the changing trends.

- Experience the results of the newly applied knowledge in the market-place.

It is constant innovation which provides an organisation the decisive competitive edge, and it is the leader's job to focus on this.

To critically look into and control the situation beneath a magnifying glass, we need to examine organisational objectives from three angles and factors which foster innovation:

1. Increase in sales

2. Increase in profitability

3. Business to become collaborative and socially inclined, taking care of all stakeholders needs

To enable all this to happen, businesses and business leaders should have both the capabilities to understand the **MIND** of the customer and develop the **METHODOLOGY** to capitalise on the changing situation.

To do this effectively, it is necessary to understand the market situation with respect to the need and demand analysis. In short, understand whether:

1. Whether your customers are being **SERVED**

2. Whether your customers are being **UNDER-SERVED**

3. Whether your customers are being **UN-SERVED**

Thus, the essence of leadership innovation is the thrust it gives to understand and efficiently serve the dynamic and changing needs of the customers.

Today, organisations need to protect and shield and arm themselves with technology. Only when the appropriate and available technology is harnessed, will organisations be alert to the context of the new economy that is constantly evolving.

But technology should not merely be used as an end by itself. Rather it should be used intelligently as a means to an end. Using technology effectively involves not being merely seduced by latest technology and forgetting the all-important 'people factor'. **Merely succumbing to competitive pressures as the reason to adopt new technology is not the done thing.**

To create a well-balanced organisation, leaders need to have an open minded approach. Being complacent by focusing on past glory will result in organisations finding themselves redundant, obsolete and out of business.

A good leader needs to take pains to explore innovative ideas, whatever be their source.

A leader who has developed his visionary eye will ensure that he as well as his organisation rise to all occasions and will create an organisation that is both sustainable and profitable.

ACTION POINTS

FROM

"मंत्र nine"

FOR YOU TO PRACTICE

1. Willingly adapt to beneficial new technologies

2. Constantly look for ways to innovate and improve

3. Set aside quality time for research and development in all areas

4. Instil the courage and thirst in your people for improving systems and processes

Your Insights...

mantra ten

DEVELOP FINANCIAL LITERACY FOR STABILITY AND SUSTAINABILITY

DEVELOP FINANCIAL LITERACY

– FOR STABILITY AND SUSTAINABILITY

ANECDOTES FROM SHIVAJI'S LIFE

Shivaji realised early on that the welfare of his people lay in the structured planning of his kingdom's resources and the rational and equitable distribution of wealth among his people.

Generating wealth for the organisation and its people by investing intelligently in various projects was the hallmark of Shivaji as a leader. He had a glorious vision as to how his kingdom should flourish. Bringing about the various conditions for his kingdom to become economically strong was always foremost in his mind.

As a great leader, Shivaji spent a considerable amount of time in creating naval bases and fortresses. Shivaji as a leader looked forward towards the betterment of his people. The chronicles speak of Shivaji's naval fleet of 700 vessels of various shapes and sizes. Most of these were mercantile or commercial vessels, used for profitable trade.

Shivaji started engaging in foreign trade with places as far away as Persia (Iran), and Basra.

Shivaji also instructed and trained his army to be self-sufficient and financially take care of itself by generating funds through military engagements.

Funds collected from the exploits of war were judiciously spent in the development of infrastructure in his kingdom. Shivaji did not just allocate funds, but also personally involved himself in the construction of the naval fortresses and other infrastructure to ensure that the funds were not wasted, but properly utilised. He ensured there was no wasteful expenditure. At the same time, funds were provided for essentials such as training for the army, and other essentials also were not ignored.

Every family in every village was expected and encouraged to contribute to the financial health of the kingdom. This was not done in an exploitative manner, but in a way where everyone benefited. If 50 kilograms of grain were contributed by a family, an equal 50 kilograms would also be given by the state as its own contribution. **This led to making villages self-**

sufficient. It also gave the citizens a sense of self-pride and feeling of contributing to their own development and also let them know that the state was there to back them up with equal support.

Such personal contribution of the people ensures the feeling of ownership and collaborative involvement and encouragement for the overall development of the organisation. This again is a concept which is important in modern management techniques, but Shivaji had put this into practice successfully over 300 years ago.

Revenue collection was done directly by the state through departments under its own control. No middlemen were allowed to milk the cream. This took effort to organise and administer, but the people benefited, and that was the main intention.

It is easy to pay and out-source and get your work done, but it takes character to take the burden of work on self - **Cyrus M Gonda, Nitin Parab**

Shivaji realised that the people who worked hard and honestly should be the true beneficiaries of the kingdom and they should be given the greater share of the financial reward. Such sound leadership thinking motivates and encourages the people. More importantly, this is the **FAIR** way to lead.

Wide-spread employment was also intelligently and consciously developed during Shivaji's rule. Army and naval personnel were also well paid. They were provided with monetary as well as non-monetary motivation.

It is a fact of life that the world today runs on money and so do all organisations, whether corporate or otherwise. So a good leader today cannot afford to be financially illiterate.

Thus Shivaji focused on good financial management so that each year the state generated a surplus which was kept in reserve to fall back on in dire times. Today's so-called 'financially literate' leaders who have led their organisations and the whole world to financial ruin by being burdened under unnecessary debt and wasteful expenditure could learn lessons in practical financial management from Shivaji Maharaj.

LEADERSHIP LEARNINGS

The visible part of modern leadership may be defined by the stirring speeches, the public appearances and so on, which the leader gives from time to time to make his presence felt. This is necessary and fine. But the true work of leadership lies behind the scene. It consists primarily of:

➤ Organising and generating resources.

➤ Taking decisions regarding resource allocation based on organisational priorities.

➤ Channelising available resources where they are most needed at the time.

➤ **Not over-spending and being lavish and extravagant, but definitely spending where**

needed – For infrastructure development, systems development, research and development, people development.

➤ Keeping sufficient resources in reserve for emergencies and contingencies.

➤ Arranging for financial liquidity when urgently needed.

➤ Understanding and analysing balance sheets.

Money is needed for almost every activity today, and a leader has to ensure that he understands and becomes smart at financial management. He should not leave the finance function in the hands of others, however reliable, knowledgeable and trustworthy they may be, without exercising some broad control over them.

This does not mean that every leader needs to be a qualified Chartered Accountant or an MBA in Finance, but he **HAS** to develop financial smartness and know-how.

This is an absolute must in today's money driven world.

It does not also mean that leaders should be getting into the nitty-gritties of day-to-day financials of the organisation and not give any financial freedom to their subordinates, by demanding that the smallest expenditure be sanctioned and approved by him alone. That is carrying things too far, and such behaviour also harms the organisation in its own way. But the leader should strike a balance in matters of financial management and should understand and take a keen interest in matters of finance as far as the organisation is concerned.

Many leaders feel shy to discuss money matters, as they feel it shows them as overly interested in financial benefits and profits. There is nothing to be shy about. This is a core part of the leader's role. It is a leaders job to think of and plan for the **'where-got'** and the **'where-gone'** of the monetary aspects of the organisation. If he does not do this vital task, who will?

Today, most organisations and even many countries find it difficult to balance budgets and are running in debts despite collecting high rates of taxes from citizens. The entire world, including the developed countries of Europe and the USA are all suffering financial crises.

Shivaji demonstrated that a good leader needs to be financially aware and provide the funds for resources necessary for running an organisation and a state.

We have recently seen too many large, well-known organisations internationally as well as in India suffer because their finances were not in order. Where suppliers have not been paid their dues and employees have not been paid their salaries. Such situations can and should be avoided by preventing them from occurring by practicing sound financial management and keeping costs and expenses within reasonable limits and clearly laying out the organisational priorities as to where money should be sanctioned first.

As Napoleon said - An army marches on its stomach.

To fill organisational stomachs, money is needed. This is something that a good leader always needs to keep in mind. This is indeed the 'practical' aspect of good leadership to ensure organisational sustainability.

ACTION POINTS
FROM
"мantra ten"
FOR YOU TO PRACTICE

1. Practice simple living and high thinking
    – These qualities identify the working
    style of a great leader

2. Develop an attitude of careful spending
    to avoid wasteful expenditure

3. Invest rightfully and lavishly in vital
    areas such as human development,
    learning and training, employee welfare,
    and customer delight

4. Learn to differentiate between what is
    an investment and what is a cost

Your Insights...

_____

_____

_____

_____

_____

_____

_____

_____

_____

_____

_____

_____

_____

Mantra Eleven

RESPECT ALL CULTURES – UNITY IN DIVERSITY WILL LEAD TO SYNERGY

RESPECT AND UNITE ALL CULTURES – GREAT LEADERSHIP APPRECIATES THE BENEFITS OF UNITY IN DIVERSITY

ANECDOTES FROM SHIVAJI'S LIFE

The Pune district during Shivaji's time was filled with hundreds of small local chieftains, each holding a village or a group of villages under their control. Most of them could not see eye-to-eye with the neighbouring chieftains, and there was a lot of conflict and misunderstanding among the various groups.

It needed a mighty man like Shivaji who had developed the quality of understanding the egos of others, to unify them to a common cause, else all the individual energies of these chieftains would have been wasted in fighting each other rather than uniting for a common objective.

Shivaji was not able to unite them merely because

he held hereditary power. He did so based on his own merit as a great leader.

He had always focused on building great strength of character based on courage and valour, and bravely took sole responsibility for his decisions. He had worked hard to earn this quality of a great leader, to unify his team for a common goal.

Shivaji was very religious minded and spiritually inclined, and he respected religious individuals from all religions, giving them the respect they deserved.

He even got constructed a *Gurudwara* in Nashik for the Sikh community.

He managed to successfully unite the chieftains of Gwalior, Indore and Baroda, and got them together on a common platform for a common cause.

Not only did he respect all religions and all cultures, but also respected all professions.

Although Shivaji was primarily a warrior, he took a great interest in the arts. The first *Urdu-Sanskrit* dictionary was compiled during his reign. He was a patron of writers, artists and musicians and they were always well received with honours at his court.

Shivaji's greatness as a **TRUE** leader of men can also be witnessed in the circumstances in which he rose to sovereignty.

He was truly an original explorer who created a new path in medieval Indian history. In front of him were very few examples or roadmaps to guide his path, but he acted truly out of divine intuition. When he chose to declare his independence, the Mughal empire appeared to be at the height of its glory. Every other local king or chieftain anywhere in India who had previously revolted against the Mughals had been crushed and vanquished.

For a person who had very little hereditary wealth except the small piece of land given him by his father, defying the resource-rich Mughals seemed to be an act of lunacy, a courting of sheer ruin.

Shivaji, however, chose this difficult path and succeeded gloriously in writing his name in golden letters across the pages of history, not only of India, but also the world.

Intensely religious from his very boyhood by instinct and training alike, he remained all through his life, free from vice, respectful to holy men, passionately fond of hearing scriptures of **all religions,** listening to sacred stories and devotional songs.

The sincerity of his character is proven by the impartial respect he had for the holy men of all sects (Hindus as well as Muslims), toleration of all caste and creed, chivalry to all women and strict morality in his camp in that age, which has even brought him admiration from critics and even historians like Khafi Khan.

He had the true leader's personal magnetism and cast a spell over all who knew him, drawing the best elements of his kingdom and from outside on his side, and winning the most devoted service from his officers. His dazzling victories and genuine ever-ready smile made him the idol of his soldiers.

The only thing he expected from his people, irrespective of their cast, creed or religion, was loyalty and devotion to the Motherland.

LEADERSHIP LEARNINGS

Respect and tolerance and acceptance of all good and loyal individuals is a prime leadership trait.

First and foremost, it shows a big heart and an open mind.

Unless the leader displays and demonstrates this trait, synergy and all the other benefits of different, diverse cultures will never accrue to the organisation.

From all cultures, there is something of value which can contribute to the success and growth of any organisation. **A good leader understands this and practices it. A good leader will welcome such diversity, provided it brings positive growth to the organisation.**

Also, in today's globalised, corporate climate, which is filled with petty egos, this is a quality which a leader cannot ignore. A true leader has to develop the art and skill of developing various sub-leaders, coming with different mind sets and from different cultural backgrounds, and unify them to a common goal and purpose.

On the point of Shivaji's patronage of artists, writers and musicians, we can compare and see that the Renaissance was a glowing period in the dark ages of European history, only because art and literature and music were encouraged and allowed to flourish.

A progressive organisation cannot survive and thrive by focusing on work alone. Intellectual and artistic development is essential for progress of the organisation and its people. Even during a reign where most of his energies were occupied in battle and in taking care of defence, Shivaji took time to encourage artists and writers and scholars. The art and literature which developed during Shivaji's reign is yet another part of Shivaji's legacy to us. **This is a quality which a leader should not neglect, however difficult the times are, as it is a sound work-life balance which is crucial to make the people more relaxed, more innovative and**

more productive. After all – 'All work and no play, make Jack a dull boy', is a very true English proverb.

Also, as a recent example of unifying people and cultures from diverse backgrounds, we can take Nelson Mandela, the first president of a free South Africa, who included a lot of whites (the members of the white race had previously treated Mandela and his native people badly), in his new leadership team. This thoughtful act built trust among the whites, and they felt they would be accepted as part of the mainstream and not be discriminated against because they were in the minority.

Nelson Mandela's brand of leadership was called 'Rainbow Leadership', as he included people of all colours, races and cultures in his core team. The world today applauds Nelson Mandela for his openness to other cultures, and it has also benefited South Africa as a nation, as all good people, irrespective of race and culture, are now joining hands and working for the progress of the country. This is primarily because Nelson Mandela gave them the clear signal that all good people, irrespective of colour and race, were needed as a vital part of the team.

Today the world applauds Nelson Mandela for his vision.

But Shivaji Maharaj had performed the same foresighted, noble gesture in his kingdom many centuries ago.

Truly, much that we need to learn about leadership is available to us from the way in which Shivaji practice his unique brand of leading.

ACTION POINTS

FROM

"ꮇantra Eleven"

FOR YOU TO PRACTICE

1. Remember, everyone from any background can collaborate and contribute to your organisation's growth and development

2. Respect every individual as a human being, first and foremost

3. Observe, identify and learn to practice the positive points from various cultures and all socio-economic backgrounds

4. Develop deep insights on cultural differences which naturally exist among various peoples and appreciate these differences in a healthy manner

Your Insights...

Mantra twelve

FOCUS ON – DELEGATION, EMPOWERMENT, SUCCESSION PLANNING

FOCUS ON - DELEGATION, EMPOWERMENT, SUCCESSION PLANNING

ANECDOTES FROM SHIVAJI'S LIFE

Shivaji well knew that the empire which he had created needed to be given in good hands. Grooming his son to take the empire forward was important for him.

Shivaji had two sons. The elder Sambhaji, and the younger Rajaram.

He decided to separate his two sons and give them different territories to govern, to test their abilities and also to inculcate in them the experience of governance which would help them in future years. This would also help them to understand the way of righteous ruling, leadership according to the Hindu religion, and the noble way of kings.

Shivaji sent Sambhaji to be mentored by the *Deputy Pandit Rao*, Keshav Bhatt. The prince was also to be directly trained in administrative matters and thus he was made governor of the Sangmeshwar district with Nilo Moreshwar (the *Peshwa's* son) as *Dewan*. At Sangmeshwar, Sambhaji attended lectures in Sanskrit, ethics and politics.

The mature leadership of Shivaji made him give away the homeland of Maharashtra with its long-settled peaceful territory and resident families of faithful hereditary ministers and generals to Rajaram, who was just a young lad of eight. The new territories captured in the south of Karnataka were given to Sambhaji because these territories needed a vigorous grown-up sovereign to secure it and for such a task it was beyond doubt due to Shivaji's clever leadership and succession planning methods that Sambhaji was the right choice.

Also, when it came to the functioning of the judiciary, Shivaji did not interfere in its working. He had delegated the authority of dispensing justice in the hands of qualified and experienced individuals and did not attempt to bias their functioning in any way.

This is why the judiciary in Shivaji's time could take correct and independent decisions without fear or favour and in the best interests of the people and of justice.

It takes great courage and self-discipline for a leader to do this. It requires an individual to develop a strong and honest character to not fall into the temptation of interfering with subordinate's decisions, once authority has been delegated, especially when one is supreme commander, and can easily do so.

Leaders of today need to develop such will power and strength of character.

Succession planning was well-understood by Shivaji. Being the son of Sahaji Raje Bhosale, Shivaji had already inherited the spirit of courage and bravery. Sahaji Raje was himself a nobleman who had fought against the atrocities committed on his people by the Mughal rulers. Sahaji Raje himself had possessed a noble and clear vision, which he passed from brave father to brave son.

Often, it takes a generation or sometimes more than one generation to fulfil a vision – **Cyrus M Gonda, Nitin Parab**

The higher and more noble the vision, the more time it could take to achieve. But the time invested will be well worth it. Remember, a tall and sturdy banyan tree takes a long time to grow to its full potential, but once fully grown, it gives shade to thousands. This is why the question of structured, organised, succession planning becomes so important a quality in a good leader. Having personally witnessed the atrocities and injustices faced by the good people of Maharashtra, Sahaji Raje, the brave father of Shivaji ignited the passion of *'Swaraj'* within Shivaji.

His father also developed in Shivaji the vision of the formation of a kingdom that allowed men to live a life of honour and respect, the only type of life really worth living.

The influence of his father and the healthy conditioning of his mind in the right direction since an early age enabled Shivaji to rise to a noble cause and establish a new way of life based on the principles of righteous living. It is due to the delegation and foresighted succession planning practiced by Shivaji and his father before him, that we today see the fruits of Shivaji's noble purpose.

LEADERSHIP LEARNINGS

Leaders in corporate houses and elsewhere need to understand that succession planning should be an integral part of their leadership responsibilities.

It is in performing this duty well that the greatness of their leadership role is established. Identifying and declaring the successive leader or leaders as per the situation, giving logical reasons and validations for any such selection, become the hallmark of visionary leadership.

Whatever the leader is able to create in his capacity of building a brand, setting up modern systems, creating a healthy environment, and so on, needs to be carried forward by others as part of a continuing

legacy. The tempo which has been set in building the organisation should never be diluted.

Just as it holds true in quantum mechanics, a body which is at rest needs more energy to bring it into action, so it is with organisations **- Cyrus M Gonda, Nitin Parab**

An organisation which is in motion requires little energy to sustain, grow and evolve. Leaving an organisation which is in the growth phase or in the matured phase in the hands of the right leader is of prime importance. Only such a leader can understand the vision and is in a better position to communicate the vision down the line to subordinates and ensure continuity of vision.

If the new leader does not have the right insights and finds it difficult to cope up with the philosophy of running an efficient organisation, then sooner or later such an organisation will fall on troubled times and will gradually fade away.

We are sure you would like to think of your organisation and your departments and units and divisions thriving and flourishing even after you hand over the reins of leadership to others at the right time.

The succession pipeline should be developed into an accountability model, wherein all aspects of leadership should be considered, so that the newly appointed leader is able to perform and execute his role successfully without any disturbances, in a smooth flow.

The leadership succession programme should resonate with change. Some of that change could happen when we observe the present leader quitting, being relieved or getting promoted to a new role. The not-so obvious change could be a change in strategy, a bad attitude, or noticeable unhappiness with the leadership requirements. This also gives an indication to pause and reflect on the course of the progress and the vision of the founders. It brings out hidden factors of the individual exploring his potential and making him take new challenges and getting them converted into effective strategies. This is the crucial time which needs to be handled well.

This time period when succession has just occurred also gives an indication to pause and reflect on the course of progress the new leader will chart for the organisation.

It brings out hidden factors of the individual exploring his potential and should make him accept new challenges, getting them converted into effective strategy.

Organisations should bring about a connective link between the various programmes that are carried out within their four walls. Leadership development training programmes need to be integrated with succession planning, performance management, competency mapping, rewards systems development and so on.

The organisational ownership component should be embedded with all leaders who are ready to take on the mantle of a decision-making role.

There should be an element of clarity among the core management team, and new leaders should be trained to understand and align with this clarity, because when there is clarity of purpose, commitment to the common cause naturally follows.

General Electric and other leading multinational organisations successfully follow these practices of succession planning today, which were put in place by Shivaji over three hundred years ago.

On the subject of delegation, Shivaji trained his subordinates to take on higher responsibilities, and at the same time he also instilled in them strong ethical values to keep in mind while carrying out their tasks and duties.

Too many leaders today delegate their jobs to people down the line without having instilled ethics and values in them to enable them to perform the delegated duties in the right manner. Lack of instilling of such values while delegating, results in discontent among stakeholders. Shivaji did not neglect this vital element before delegating tasks to his subordinates.

A good leader understands the need for thoughtful delegation. He is on a constant vigil to see that his VISION gets encrypted into the minds of his people and synchronised with the emotions of the workforce so that he is left relatively free to grow the business and look into areas of pressing matters, such as dealing with the effects of competition and rapid globalisation.

But when authority is delegated to individuals who are immature and unprepared for it, corruption and mismanagement result.

Leaders should nurture and develop, not hand-hold and spoon-feed their subordinates – **Cyrus M Gonda, Nitin Parab**

Let subordinates develop in the right and natural way by giving them the opportunity to make correct decisions, after instilling in them the right values and providing them the necessary support systems.

Good leaders should also support the decisions of their subordinates which are made with good intent. They should compliment and appreciated the process, and not merely the results, as it is the following of proper processes which develops good leaders.

Subordinates to whom the task is delegated should be made to realise that results obtained by by-passing correct procedure are not acceptable, and would harm the organisation in the long run. This fact should be ingrained in their minds before tasks are delegated. Then only is the process of delegation completed.

The great need of the hour in our organisations and in our nation today is the development of good, sound leaders at all levels in the hierarchy.

The lessons corporate houses need to take from this learning is that succession planning should be an integral part of the leadership spectrum. Here, the greatness of the existing leader is established.

Declaring the successive leader or leaders as per the situation and requirement with validation for any such choice, becomes the hallmark of visionary leadership.

Whatever the leader is able to create in his capacity of building a brand, setting up modern systems, creating a holistic environment, etc., needs to be carried on as part of his legacy.

The society of tomorrow will not be able to bear the enormous fallacies and the whimsical natures of those untrained for leadership positions. There should be an element of clarity amongst the top-core team, because only with clarity of purpose will commitment and long-term success naturally follow.

Thus this quality of a leader is of prime importance, as too often we have seen great work done by a leader washed away after he is no more with the organisation, as he did not take steps to identify and groom the appropriate successors for future leadership roles in the organisation.

Just practice and invest substantial time in developing this quality of succession planning, and half your work as a leader is complete.

ACTION POINTS

FROM

mantra twelve

FOR YOU TO PRACTICE

1. Delegate intelligently so that you as a leader are free to take on higher levels of responsibility

2. Train and develop your people to primarily think as leaders

3. Encourage your people to take informed decisions

4. Empower your people to think and take actions for the primary benefit of the organisation

Your Insights...

_____

_____

_____

_____

_____

_____

_____

_____

_____

_____

_____

_____

_____

мantra thirteen

LEAVE A LASTING LEGACY FOR FUTURE GENERATIONS TO BUILD ON

LEAVE BEHIND A SOUND LEGACY FOR ORGANISATIONAL CONTINUITY

ANECDOTES FROM SHIVAJI'S LIFE

Shivaji is fondly remembered by all patriotic Indians, just as the Romans remember Julius Caesar, the French remember Emperor Napoleon, and the Greeks remember Alexander the Great.

Ten thousand years from today, the memory of Shivaji will burn as pure and bright and continue to inspire and motivate Indians to sacrifice their today for a better tomorrow.

Leadership definitely offers privileges, but correspondingly demands certain sacrifices as well from the leader. It is these very sacrifices he makes, which make a leader remembered for all time, and not the privileges which the leader gained and benefited from while he was in power.

When vision is clear, and effort is supreme, and sacrifice is voluntary, a lasting legacy is created – **Cyrus M Gonda, Nitin Parab**

So too in the case of Shivaji, who thought extremely long-term and acted accordingly. In fact, Shivaji has been considered by historians to be the prime architect of *Swaraj* (Indian Independence). **Many have described Shivaji as an Avatar (Godly reincarnation); as a divine being born on this earth for a noble purpose for a noble cause.**

Shivaji paved the way for India's ultimate unification by lighting the patriotic spark in the minds and hearts of the Indian people. This is his legacy for the Indian people for which we are all eternally grateful.

Starting his journey with virtually no inherited property apart from a small *jagir* (piece of land), with a few caretakers, Shivaji was a self-made man, leaving behind as his legacy many forts, a strong, well-trained army and navy, an effective system of justice and administration, and most importantly, he left behind in his people the spirit to live lives filled with a noble purpose. This was Shivaji's legacy to the great Indian nation and to his people. Of course, needless to say, Shivaji was gifted with the blessings of his parents and mentors which made this possible.

Shivaji's strength lay in the ability to articulate his vision clearly and ably to his people, making them rise above the average, thereby making them perform at their best potential, which is the invaluable legacy that a true leader gifts his people.

Shivaji's nobility of character, his love for his people and his concern for their welfare, and his devotion to the sacred soil of the motherland, are not only fondly remembered today, but will be worshipped till this world remains.

He communicated a clear cause and made ordinary individuals rise to extraordinary heights to pursue that noble cause.

Because Shivaji had ensured sound structure in hierarchy and administration, which was built on merit and performance and not on sycophancy and yes-man-ship, the great Maratha empire which Shivaji established was able to sustain and flourish after him under the Peshwas, who were not his blood relatives, but could run the kingdom with patriotic zeal and passion and commitment, because Shivaji had established systems for continuing his sound legacy forward.

Shivaji built a nation. He laid the foundation not only of a kingdom, but also of a war-machine which could cater to any circumstances or conditions brought about by hostile enemies.

It was the art of nation-making that Shivaji envisaged, for which he is rightly revered and remembered today.

LEADERSHIP LEARNINGS

The actions which a leader performs with good intent, set in motion a cosmic chain of events which culminate and see their fulfilment at a later date. It is like the noble man planting trees for future generations to benefit from.

Similarly, at a time when all over Hindustan, dark clouds of foreign rule dominated, Shivaji Maharaj was the bright ray of sunshine which kept the territory under his control free from foreign rule.

All patriotic individuals could find refuge to rest, recuperate and re-energise under Shivaji's protective hand. This too is Shivaji's legacy.

Similarly for leaders today, it is important that they provide a safe and secure oasis and haven for their people to rest, recuperate, and then once again, after having recharged their energies, the people can re-enter the front line with renewed vigour to perform their tasks with dedication and devotion.

It is a sad fact that in most organisations today, leaders are unable to motivate their people to perform at their best. In fact, surveys in corporate houses have shown that about 50 percent of new employees lose their motivation to perform within 15 days of their joining, as the motivation to perform for a noble cause is not forthcoming from the leaders of these organisations. Most managers today are too caught up in petty organisational politics and micro-management to have the time and energy for organisation building.

We earnestly beseech all of you reading this book to pay homage to Shivaji's memory and practice the leaving behind of a sound legacy for future generations your main priority as a leader.

May Chhatrapati Shivaji Maharaj's blessings be with you on your leadership journey.

ACTION POINTS

FROM

"मantra thirteen"

FOR YOU TO PRACTICE

1. Always remember, the organisation is bigger than any individual, and should last longer than the life of any individual associated with it

2. Gainfully keeping people profitably employed is one of the most noble objectives of a leader

3. Leaders should invest sufficient time in developing successors who will work for the long-term benefit of the organisation

4. Encourage promotion to key positions from within the organisation

Your Insights...

_____

_____

_____

_____

_____

_____

_____

_____

_____

_____

_____

Profile - Cyrus M Gonda

Cyrus is a MENSA member, and loves reading and writing.

He is interested in the areas of literature, mythology, history and geography, and is always on the lookout for interesting anecdotes related to countries, corporate houses, and individuals.

He enjoys relating these anecdotes to current problem areas in the corporate world, and attempts to provide solutions for current issues through past and present benchmarks.

He is regarded as a thought-leader in management circles and has co-authored many cutting edge management books with his colleague, Dr Kalim Khan, including : "Where Is My Ketchup ?", "Seal The Hole In The Bucket", and "Be A Super Salesperson".

PROFILE – Dr. Nitin Parab
Qualifications: BE, MBA, PGDAPR, MS, PhD

Nitin, a Corporate Warrior with 20 years of experience is the CEO & Evangelist at Crosslink International, a strategic HR and Leadership Training firm.

Prior to Crosslink International, Nitin was the youngest Chief Operating Officer at Sakal Infotek and Sakal Printers, part of the Sakal Group. He has established 2 schools of Yoga and imparted knowledge to more than 10,000 individuals.

Nitin is an avid reader of Leadership & Management books trying to decipher the link between ethical human behavior and performance in the world of business. He has written for various newspapers and currently is a regular column writer with the BSE Forum on Leadership Insights.

He is a keynote speaker at various business forums and management institutes.

His Goal is to create the Divine Leadership mindset so that the organizations of the future are based on strong Human Values, Ethics, Trust and Optimum

Energy. He believes that the world can experience Peace and Harmony through an economic renaissance brought about by the goodness in Human Nature and Spirit.

His new training program to the Corporate world on YogLeadership is a rightful blend of Change Management Mindset and Personal Evolvement.

ONE DAY WORKSHOP –
"Mastering Leadership Mantras"

The authors, Cyrus and Nitin's One-Day Workshop entitled – "Mastering Leadership Mantras" is conducted for participants to understand beneficial leadership traits, create leaders through succession planning, and enhance organisational culture.

Workshop Highlights:

- Know your Mind-set so that you can lead effectively.

- Understand, Communicate, Demonstrate – Leadership

- Create a Vision Roadmap and align Thoughts with Actions.

- Understand the Emotional Quotient of Leadership

- Build Trust through Effective Communication

- Understand Temple Yoga and the Art of Re-energising

- Adopt the Role of a Mentor

- Empower your People and create Winning Teams
- Leave a Lasting Legacy

Who would Benefit by Attending this Workshop:
- Junior, mid-level and senior managers who are leading teams
- Start-up entrepreneurs
- Campus students eager to make a mark as future leaders

Contact for Attending Workshop :
nitinp@crosslinkint.net

Printed in Great Britain
by Amazon

48227368R00081